MEANDERING THROUGH TIME

VOLUME 2

MEANDERING THROUGH TIME

VOLUME 2

by

Bruce Parry

Bruce Parry

Moyhill Publishing

First Published in 2021 by Moyhill Publishing

ISBN 978-1-913529-81-9

A CIP catalogue record for this book
is available from the British Library.

Cover design and typesetting by *Moyhill* Publishing.

Moyhill Publising,
1965 Davenport House, 261 Bolton Rd, Bury, Gtr. Manchester BL8 2NZ UK.

Dedication

This second book is dedicated to my late mother June Theresa Parry (1925 – 2006). An artist in every sense of the word, a painter, wordsmith, actress and costumier of very skilled natural ability. She had the remarkable talent of connecting to so many different people in all walks of life, indeed, sacrificing much in helping others to find their way through complicated times. This book is for her, and I hope it will be special for many people reading it in all walks of life also.

Contents

Introduction

Well, it's hard to believe 2021 has arrived, we are in the second year of a world pandemic of the Covid-19 virus, this situation has spurred me on to continue my passion for writing, and yes, this dire world event has once again reinforced my belief that creativity is everything. I'm continuing my theme of Meandering Through Time, Volume 2. It was incredibly difficult to choose the pieces included here, but my prime objective is always to both entertain and connect to just ordinary people, therefore, please join me on this thought provoking journey…the clock is ticking. Within these pages you will find much reference to childhood, adolescence and adult yearning focused on our endearing connection to the natural world around us.

I hope you will enjoy this second volume of 'Meandering Through Time' as much as I have enjoyed writing and creating it.

All similarities of names, dates and observations are purely coincidental and fictitious as part of the creative story telling process except for the reference to artist J.M.W. Turner in 1844, 'Rain, Steam and Speed, the Great Western Railway in the piece 'Painted Boats.'

Bruce Parry.

Sky Train

There is a feeling of release and freedom
inside this rainbow
It is quiet and peaceful, but slightly wet,
I'm not obligated here, within these colours
It is simple and less noisy, I'll stay.
Not slide down into that pot of gold, too complicated!
The rainbow understands me, even in thunder
These colours magnify green on earth, blue on sea,
"Will this rainbow end soon? I hope not!"
But the chalk drawings on pavements
will run away in downpours
And will the lightening photograph them
into memory?
Other rainbows will cross the sky…
new sky trains for my ride to freedom.

Ivy Creep

Ivy creep tells of age
Insidious, green and tangled,
Twisting along gutters
Engulfing crumbling brick,
Clinging to the last moments of shady green
That was once pebble dash perfect,
Ivy creep moves forward with ticking clocks
Each leaf a second, each root a year,
A lifetime of growing moves under roof tiles
Eating soft timbers, that were once
tree like and wind blown,
Ivy creep climbs castles and towers
Hiding Rapunzel from passing Princes
Who are always riding in woodland
Where witches live who cackle with crows,
But ivy still creeps and climbs slowly
Caressing holly sharp and mistletoe kissed,
To the sound of distant village bells
Inside churches that are Christmas lit,
Where ivy creeps outside in mist
Clinging to gravestones, that tell of ages past,
Still insidious, green and tangled.

Pylon

May came into bloom suddenly, nodding flowers exchanged their flowing currency...

Church bells chimed across the yellow rape, red poppies bobbed in between...growing their sadness once again...

How could it be so bright? Beyond, a puffy sky met a straight stark sea, a breeze whistled through the wired...harp like fences...

Pylons marched across the land, clutching their humming cables, relentless and tall...

As if travelling over hill and dale, towards some kind of unknown armageddon, powering our computers and devices...

We sit silently at the other end staring at our screens, unaware of our decline and loss of control, as we are fed more and more artificial intelligence...

The steel giants tread the landscape, dip into valleys, rise across rivers, buzz over lost woodland and reflect hot sun...

The land is patchwork with wild and tidy colourful days, night folds down and keeps it safe in silhouette, until dawn breaks it free…

May came into bloom suddenly, and was bright, wild deer jumped over hedgerows and gathered in woodland that was magical again.

Unicorn Prince and Princess...

Persian Princess, a dulcimer she played
For the loss of her Prince, who would have stayed,
But departed at night to the woodland glade
Where unicorns danced in silvery shade,
Magic on earth was watery drenched
Where grew haunted trees of roots intrenched,
They spoke to the Prince, but made no sense
In the language of trees... that was past tense,
The Princess followed to the woodland glade
Her dulcimer singing under the silvery shade,
She sat beneath the trees... of roots intrenched
Singing to the leaves with her dulcimer lent...
...on her knees, as the trees, swayed in sweet time,
The blow of the breeze keeping in rhyme
And telling of her Prince in the Unicorn land,
In a language the Princess could truly understand.
As she plucked the strings, a Unicorn sat
With a saddle of moss and hooves of black,
The Princess floated up onto it's elegant back
Riding like a fairy into the forest track.
This dulcimer maid was happy at last
On a quest for her Prince...in a forest of the past.

Planting Nature –
A Walk In The Woods

It's when I went off track across a wild bit that I found a full sized walnut tree...just on it's own, not with others, just on it's own...just there in the middle...on it's own standing proud, surrounded by other trees...trees you find in the woods.

How did it get there, when did it germinate, this is a big tree laden with autumn walnuts, how old we can only guess? Did people live nearby, once upon a time...in an old cottage or shack perhaps, where nature hid its foundations? Where leaves and leaf mould piled up and crumbled everything to dust... where nature finally won over brick and wood and now it's just this tree left standing with no clues?

I call it planting nature...the apple core that gets thrown from a train window. It rolls and jumps down the embankment with its pips falling away to be buried in the rain and mud...and one finally grows, tiny and struggling. Thousands and thousands of trains will pass by and the one core that was thrown will grow. Those rosy reds that we look down at from the train will drop to the ground...how did those apple trees get there…down there on the windswept embankment, where nobody can get to?

I do it all the time now, I hope every apricot stone I throw into the river will travel to remote places and self germinate in perfect mud or silt miles and miles away…other people will wonder how that apricot tree got to the edge of the woods, after all those years… growing quietly, surrounded by other trees…trees you find in the woods.

I came across a huge damson tree hanging over a canal…branches almost snapping with the weight of damsons which were fed and fed from the water, from the silt and mud. Did a damson stone land here from holiday boaters on the canal coming from London and beyond? A kilo of damson stones thrown into the water, all travelling down river to find their place to grow…the cherry stones, peaches, greengage and more, all travelling down river to plant nature…surrounded by other trees…trees you find in the woods.

The abandoned tramway, where Sunday school picnics threw apple and pear cores into the passing woodland…where birds pecked and carried pips from tree to tree, depositing them in manure where they grew beyond Sunday school lives, beyond the tramway, way past years that closed villages. And the trees thrived…on the edge, in the woods, behind old walls. Where cottages once stood called Mulberry and Cherry Tree, Hazel End and Appleby Halt… and the children waved from the trams, where they were given fruit for the picnics from ancient cottage gardens and allotments, surrounded by other trees… trees you find in the woods.

Travelling Fair

Rain the night before had merged its summer layer, on parkland sweet...

Tyres on trucks carrying secret rides, had sunk into ridges still to be trodden...

Showmen moved bolts and stanchions in complicated directions...

The fair had arrived, coal puffed since dawn, from moonlight travels...

Even the trees seemed to bend in watching sway, as colours were built...

The park would stay awake for three days plus two, for carnival revels...

Fresh paint smell drifted towards a caravan bright, where laced curtains lived...

Park keeper stern patrolled the edge and smiled at swing boats, still rain dripped empty...

Nearby narrow boats arrived at canal's edge, bringing coal to fire the thrills and fury...

Offloading into carts, drawn by horses that knew bridges and tunnels, roped together...

The smell of coal, steam and melting sweet toffee merged with organ music bright, bright as brass...

Red neck ties and flat caps identified each showman, lifting and sifting slack to feed the mechanics of pleasure...

Open topped horse drawn carts brought the multitudes of brolly maidens and children sailor dressed to the park entrance, moustached men helped them down steps to walk towards a paradise Edwardian sweet...

The switchback ride bumped over it's wooden tracks, up and down over gentle hills of thrill...

Seats like thrones held suits and straw boaters, long dresses and wide hats brimmed with blooms, and children bobbing, all like stiff wrapped presents...

Toffee apples held tight, smooth and sugar sweet, moved through the crowds of new money luxury, and pretty hula hoops to roll along with a stick won from coconut shy and hook the duck...

The hand turned chair-o-planes spun children outwards in dizzy delight, whilst Punch and Judy

crashed wood on wood with bright painted cheeks
and fixed eyes…of delight and fright…!

The helter-skelter towers above like a lighthouse
sturdy, overlooking a moving mass of wood and
steel, the fortune teller automata churns out cheap
one farthing tickets, she will know the future as her
head turns and eyes look forward…

Boys in muddy boots will become soldiers, girls
in white ankle boots will become nurses, time will
stop the carousel…and the engines will grind on to
mechanised horror…

… "And we could not tell them."

In memory of the Great War…
before the world stopped in 1914.

Maple Red

*The maple leaves are dark red now, with the colour
of conflict...
But the tree continues to grow and spread, as does
conflict...
The leaves will fall to ground, weaving another
carpet of conflict and war...
And so it goes, and so it grows...and the graves will
be deeper...
... covered in maple red.*

Painted Boats

Gentle hands paint wooden boats with roses and castles depicted high on green rocky hills that are not on canals, beautifully scripted in shiny paint, ornate and scrolled, precise and water edged...

Stove hands cook and clean inside the Butty, white smocked and lace bonnet in fumes of a coal burning smoke stack, that drifts across rowan high and tangled hawthorn...

Horses pull with polished brass through and over bridges of heavy tow, rough callous hands groom and brush them sublime for days journey...

The canal is thick with weed, narrow boats cut through with pointed destination during summers growth whilst ducks swim in convoy, better than coal engines and tillers tangled...

Children man the towpath horses, navi built pathways of perfection, still unsullied and smooth by canal edge made strong, where digging deep styled this Utopian waterway of commerce and dreams...

Hands with picks and shovels toiled sunrise to sunset, a Victorian workforce larger than any history after the pyramids, dug deep and long, bricked and cemented for life, married in water…

The waterways were born for gypsy rovers, travellers and cargo that moved life through locks, windless hands wound up and down in time for schedules bringing coal, milk, steel, pottery, wood and ice blocks for a new consumer generation…

Boat children picked hedgerow food with tiny hands grasping at natures bounty for stews to sustain and fill forever hungry needs…

Mothers found their way to the maternity canal hospitals near schools, where unkempt working children learned a little before moving on through lock flights to profit, from goods and chattel when living was hard and unremembered in painted scenes…

Rough hands guided the ropes around newly painted bollards, whilst locks rise upwards to the next level past heavy gates as moonlight beamed for horse feeding and mooring time, stew with cabbage tops, consumed around coal stoves snug…

Pipe smoke from tobacco tin coveted…absorbs itself into woodwork memory, built by hands that smooth and etch interior living in tiny spaces, a window out with doors closed inwards, keeping precious bread safe inside, through night and day…

Miles away, on Thames skiffs, white suited men in straw boater hats and long dressed women in frills and sun brollys drink champagne in crowded locks, as Sunday speaks of outings and flirtations, secret and hands held in coy demure, whilst the uniformed lock master surveys his rising monied flock…

His tanned hands release the sluice gates, the already drunken revellers bob from side to side with lock filling undercurrents, knocking over bottles and over dressed ladies like skittles…

Sunday on the water was the new church of a post Great War generation, dedicated to excess and liberty after insurmountable losses on battle fields, far away from Thames meadows and fine houses with buttercup lawns that touched lapping water…

Hands were the life force of canal building, the boats that sailed on them with their painted dreams and the cranes that lifted cargo to feed the choking black skies of the industrial revolution…

The wooden narrow boats rotted away making way for metal steam driven replacements, hands painted them pretty again, bold and shiny, passing on the dream to the descendants who knew locks, bridges, loud weirs and hedgerows that had grown high…

In 1844, J.M.W. Turner lifted and held his brushes

to depict 'Rain, Steam and Speed, the Great Western Railway, trains would finally decimate the hands that lovingly painted boats, their roses and castles and the horses that slept silently on tow paths where water lapped through rushes…

Simple

I'm happy by the sea, in my unhappiness
A lighthouse blinks, in the blink of an eye,
Leaving the moon to reflect scurrying crabs
That hide under seaweed umbrellas.

This tidal world moves against consistent rocks
That stand alone collecting smoothness,
Becoming my stepping stones for youth
Where I jumped with show off shouts.

The sea is my marker, when simple changed
To hands held complexity, and eyes shone,
Bright and steady, in hats held windy
Past boating lake ropes, "Come in No. 6!"

This sea is my sea, the world of my oyster
A pearl to love, as the tide moves sideways,
The rotting jetty is a skeleton of old sea
Where boats and nets tangled, side by side.

Stones are heaped, where power stacks them
Twice daily, for tidiness and new dawns,
I will look and say, "This is the sea, my sea"
Turning back, shrieking gulls will confirm, "My sea."

When the tide is out, I want it to come home
Bubbling towards a lone Punch and Judy box,
Applauding it's bright, stand alone stripes
Just above the paddling of tiny feet that sink.

Bigger feet will walk these shores and sink
Heads full of dreams, scrambled with age,
Ah! The sea, it's salt and talking shells
That came from far away, chattering up the sand.

I'm happy by the sea, in my unhappiness
The sea is my marker, when simple changed,
This sea is my sea, the world of my oyster
Collecting shells, that came from far away.

Sudden Summer

Birds on aerials hop from prong to prong, almost
gathering for a Hitchcock finale

A neighbours paddling pool, no longer silent,
screams children and hosepipe cold,

Mrs. Edwards on the other side, is straw hatted for
her Miss. Marple flower tending and a book to read
for summer teas.

A distant transistor radio sings 'Help Me Rhonda'
from beaches far away when ice creams melted into
soda pop,

There is music that is summer and only belongs there,
with lost loves and fairgrounds in parks.

The tea houses built in woodland...made of wood
from woodland, are tea urn ready, for meandering
walkers and children that have built fearne camps in
secret places under shady trees.

Bold red tractors move through narrow lanes past
the edges of picnic revels, where pickles crunch with
cucumber cool.

The fields move away to a distant patchwork kingdom, alive with colour, as summer dictates…

The sea is further, where rock gardens grow flowers in equal numbers to weeds, that should have been weed free…long before the flower clock bloomed.

Rose garden petals have blown away to make perfume with sea air…where new love was born, hand in hand, ice cream and ice cream.

The grass has grown under my feet again, beauty and lilacs have caught me out…in this sudden summer.

August Rush

Rain now, falling straight, in an August rush to the end...

Cobwebs stretched across grass gleam in fading sun, where deer tread in Spring...

A morning chill tells of deeper rabbit holes and squirrels collecting quickly on bowed branches...

Flowers are closing, a finale of Autumn creeping towards their colours...

The holly bushes stand brave, in readiness for their evergreen winter solstice...

A lone rook chatters of this new dawn, as moon drops fade into mist...

Our clocks tick relentlessly, as twigs and leaves fall from a dry summer...

And the retribution of bold winds will scatter its moving targets...

Heaped up and rain sodden, before frosts crisp them up for bonfires bright…

Rain now, falling straight, in an August rush to the end…and Autumn moves slowly towards us.

Seascape

Autumn had arrived in a blowing seascape,
A clothes line swings with faded pegs in a
skeleton dance.
Seaside sand castles have dissolved with
melted ice cream,
Boarded up boarding, breakfast
8.00am till 9.30 prompt.
Don't be late for the dining room view
and rain swept August days,
Ever hopeful retirement endings,
winter shingle strewn promenade.
Trousers rolled high with sandy tip toed
fish and chips,
Light up nights of fairy lights and happy valley paths,
Curving into the dark of lovers places.
Barnacle decorated and disillusioned pier
stretches out to sea.
It's salt, it's seagull cry, it's busy past, walking past,
Warm prom, worn prom, see you next year prom,
neater than last year prom.
"Has the town slumped into slumber, or am I older?"
Tarnished and all seeing, noticing the chipped paint
on cast iron columns of glass roofed Victoriana,
Long grass and sand dunes, sand blowing and wind
stinging on the café windows.

Snug inside with our frothy coffee, bucket and spade,
comic books and threepenny laughing policeman
inside a glass case.
We walked home, climbing the hill to our board...
Looking back at distant lights that beckon our fair-
ground youth, donkey riding, a tram ride and
candy floss love...
...before Autumn had arrived in a blowing seascape.

Gone Home

Autumn leaves fall onto the already fallen, kicking, crunching boots on legs of solid people and the wind blows them along…

Tattered bunting flaps along the seagull cries, seaside days fall away with the leaves and rusty fire escapes…

Vacancies peer through the dim lit windows of B & B proud, as the tide advances. White topped waves are animated by a smiling moon that looks down at a final display of fairy lights…

Cardboard boxes and strewn rubbish fill end of season bins, beach hut shutters are closed and padlocked to protect tiny worlds inside, tiny worlds that might come back…

A cool wind spirals down the helter-skelter, where rustic mats moulted from April to September, pink haired and stick like candy floss girls have shuttered down…

Homeward bound to white sugar in tea, corn flakes and icing on a Christmas cake in a quiet town, a town watched from above only by the stars and gulls…

Holiday romances have left on their separate trains, each destination unknown to each other, each station announcement lost into the rain swept glass roof...

The long pier glints with it's dominance and sturdy iron, whilst the waves continue painting it rust and decorating with seaweed ornaments...

The tide will leave and return, bringing more paint and ornaments, eating into iron and concrete and bringing more shells for next year's children and buckets...

The B & B's stand defiant, no sand in the rooms, but the wind and shoes bring more, it creeps, it seeps, finding home, even after the jolly coaches have departed...

Vacuum cleaners stand ready, they toil to a sandy end, where motors burn out and stop, the relentless wind in the dunes will not...

Fishermen will fill the pier now, where fairground rides sparked and shunted the screams, they come from inland afar, with rods and boxes and seats and shelters...

Away from drilling, hammers, painting, furniture kits and bin day, their rods pointing out to the windmills and horizon beyond, beyond this pier of boards and dreams…

The ghost train is empty of cars, wind drift blows through the hanging skeletons, it's emptiness haunted by the siren like sound of the waves below…

Tom and Shelley, Richard and Toni, Sarah and Gillian and little Spencer, have all screamed and laughed in the darkness, thrown sideways and holiday kissed…

Ghosts have hibernated into warm central heating behind front doors, lighted windows and sheds that lock…

The ghost train stands alone, with the skeletons and fishermen with rods, boxes and tobacco…

The 'Art Deco' cinema's concrete is cracked and crumbling, once a final shining destination with a restaurant above, for before and after supper…

Even masonary paint cannot stop this wind and salt, seaside skirts and jeans sat watching a black and white wonder, with chocolates and neat hair…

A late night Dracula film, with hands held innocent by the sea, arms around each other with chips and walking back through the fairy light grotto to their secret room, warm skin and hair that tumbles down from tight comb grips…

Autumn leaves fall onto the already fallen, kicking, crunching, boots on legs of solid people, and the wind blows them along.

Harvest Moon

Orange cloaked spiritual moon watches over our witching hours,

Following a lifetime of harvest festivals and the smell of fresh fruit in our childhood churches.

It's giant orange form guards the crop circles and sheaves of corn standing alone, before the rains come.

High above the horizon, it watches our bonfires with approval, before we light our elemental offerings.

This rolling moon with her half smile, lights our way in darkness, following us home,

A lantern we know, but are still not sure of when we walk past the whispering trees.

Harvest moon, it's arrival reminding us that time has unrolled another year, diminishing our best efforts,

Orange cloaked spiritual moon, watches over our witching hours.

Autumn's Children

Autumn's children walk softly through villages of coloured toadstools that peep through crunchy leaves...

Collecting sticks that will become magic wands, to be dried and painted for sparring spells in the gardens of youth...

A sun glints down through almost bare trees, sharing the sky with a kind moon with a rocky face that knows it's children...

These two celestial giants bring Autumn's children into a perfect triad of brightness...

This time of changing leaves will be a colour pallet that was never meant for the children of Spring and Summer...

But Autumn's children will move forward into Winter, rock steady, knowing twisted trees that will soon be snow white and leaning...

Autumn will light up these children in a chestnut glow, on fires that burn sap with heated red coals...

Frost will surround the children of dark nights, and the world will love them...for their magical birth.

Conker Time

*Wind and rain push the branches of horse-chestnut
to scatter childhood across the land,
green shells break open to reveal the promising
brown shine,
tiny wellingtons jump and squash them apart for
chestnut gold.*

*Conkers slide out from their green summer coats
gleaming with Autumn,
finding sticks to throw up to knock down bigger ones,
they fall like sky treasure, prickly and tumbling,
tread of heavy bags full, across an empty park.*

*Where crunchy leaves are stacked in bonfire piles,
by Park Keepers that rake and smile with teeth
gripped pipes,
tobacco waft drifts along with the dancing leaves,
that will burn bright before a Christmas wish.*

*Children fall into the leaf stacks that remain so dry,
so high,
losing hats and boots in laughter and daring,
and homeward bound with conkers to sort and
skewer the holes,*

*threading with string that must be strong and
knotted twice,
for battles in playgrounds with drinking fountains,
and corners where milk crates are stacked,
hands sting from 'sixer' misses before the playtime
bell.*

*The half term moon is so large and bright,
shining down on the bag of conkers left behind, by
the back door,
forgotten and last to become wet and mouldy,
finally thrown on the bonfire for spitting and crackle,
flaming light that reflects in Guy Fawkes's masks.*

*Raked over days later,
one conker survives and rolls down into ash,
buries itself in rain and germinates among the
houses,
growing tall, unheeded, in a new garden.*

*Wind and rain push the branches of horse-chestnut
to scatter childhood across the land…and the stories
will be told again…*

Bonfire Memories

We look up in awe of your height,

The complexity of criss cross twigs brought by us,

Piling you high with tinder, anticipating the thrill of it,

You crackled and glowed, telling of bonfires past and present, as you warmed the cold holly.

Glowing ash sparks in twisting flight, billowing smoke we tried to avoid, but stayed anyway.

Our faces warmed and shining, as we stood before our frosted garden heating pyre.

Guy Fawkes guy, newspaper stuffed, unread, soon crackling and gone, dust bound, as children danced around you, absorbing your power.

You burned Witches, Heretics and Sorcerers, and knew their souls well, their innocence forked in ash. Raked and added to, warming us longer, black and smouldering, we poked and prodded with burnt end sticks, content of your job well done.

Brightly dimming in your corner of the world, you sleep now, we sleep, while all around you grows more fuel, for our childrens' children.

A Walk In The Park –
The Children's Mission and
Advent Church 1938–1939

A brass plaque mounted and firm on the Mission wall, tells of the lost children abandoned, and the parents trapped in life, drink and poverty on the hard road of existence…

There was no large garden or open space at the inner – city Mission and Church, just Sunday school and those walks in the park on structured outings and special holiday days…

The snaking lines of children, white socked, brown sandalled, short trousered and scrubbed carbolic. Hats Sunday school tilted with scarves striped and tucked for a day out, they trail towards the gated entrance that is open and heaven, green leafed, rolling grass and places to hide…

The park keeper stands ready to meet and greet teachers and brethren carers, pushed along out of their depth by the voices and breath of the mass, clutching excited colouring books and crayons that will become rainbows of pictures and castles…egg and cress marked and day out dog eared…

War has not marked these children yet, only the twisting of life and luck in a 1930's England, where Will Hay and Gracie Fields rule the silver screen, front gardens are rose petalled, shopkeepers sweep pavements at end of day, coal lorries deliver black and the radio talks it's music...

Dog walkers are left standing aside as the groups fill the pathways, swing and recreation bound, where roundabout and see-saw are green and red, bolted down in concrete with 11.00 o' clock just a swish, twirl and knee scrape away...

Girls with ribboned bunches, gaps where teeth will come, fly on swings like parachutes, chains held tight and lean back tighter. Boys now untucked, run like Indians pulling the roundabout faster and faster around, fully loaded with the fatter boy and all of the thin that are the braves that sit...

The park encompasses this collective of small and starting out, and will watch over them in years to come, and how the years will fly, and how the clock will tick through war torn evacuation, their return will be teenage and different, too much older for the Children's Mission and Advent Church, destroyed in 1940, but later re-built in 1947...

But today is bright, the sun shatters the leafy green trees that whisper reassurance and endless playtime.

Re-assembled and slightly tidy, the children are lined and move onwards to the river and the old bridge for picnicking. Sitting on mounds of bumpy grass in favoured groups, unwrapping sandwiches and snacks, where the sound of the flowing silver river battles to compete with the cackle and laughter that has moved in and taken the river to task...

Lunch scoffed and apple cores floated away on the water wide under the bridge like Pooh sticks, the children are re-assembled, lined and mustered along into unwanted boy, girl, boy, girl divisions, over the bridge to the toilets and the brand new model village that awaits their Gulliver trails...

Built as a new 'park attraction' and tribute to the local town during a period of 1930's opulence and wealth, this model village would spawn many others in a post WW1 England. Inside, miniature worlds through a turnstile entrance of fresh paint, red and slate roofs, church steeples, roads and school buildings, street lamps, petrol pumps, shops with windows and little people, the occasional car and lorry, cattle market, playground with gates and real pavements...

Babbling and excited, in awe of this new wonder tinier than themselves, kneeling down and peering into windows and doors with secret worlds inside, the smell of new wood and rooftops that shine in the sun, the green of tiny trees and hedges, the blue of the duck pond and white of the puddle ducks in a line…a green England before the air raids and where the rubble stacks opened up the sky, where roses grew next to neat hedges and straight fences…and where children played war and guns…

Single file now through exit turnstile and across the park to the empty bandstand, colouring books, pencils and crayons arrive from shiny satchels as the children sit in perfect circles of reverence and order to draw and colour the day…

Their musical chattering in bursts of symphonic harmony, balancing the accidentals of the finest composition that a brass band might have played here on any given church walk Sunday morning…

The sun was sliding down the sky as the children walked in now tired dishevelled lines across a park where once again, Autumn would fall from the trees after this endless summer…

The children of the Advent Church and Mission were hastily evacuated in 1939, the first air raids destroyed the buildings in 1941, it was years later when the rubble was being cleared that they found the burnt edged drawings titled 'A Walk in the Park' scattered around the dormitories…

Scrawled crayon drawings of stick giants towering over houses, eyes peering through windows, big puddle ducks with little people, scribbles of children with sandwiches and apples, ponds with crooked yachts on them, swings and slides overloaded with thin children and aeroplanes coming through the sky…

A brass plaque, mounted and firm on the new Advent Church and Mission wall tells of the evacuated children, their lives, their drawings…and their walks in the park dressed for Sunday best.

Photographs In The Lost Year

We have taken less photographs in recent times in this year of blank, we look towards an older time of albums and dusty tired tins, stacked full of misty out of focus people we never met or do not know, black and white, colour and movie films lost in albums and spools, so far back and so many, we'll never sort them out.

Scenes of a grey day picnic, kettle boiling on a leaning Primus stove, shivering but smiling through with their first motor car behind them, included with pride in front of a lay by gravel pile, but hoping to be home soon to the leg of joint in the oven in tidy suburbia away from cold bleak.

A distant auntie, with thick black spectacles rocking a last generation pram, baby included, who once paddled in Margate and decided to live there because of it, far away from white step scrubbed, laced windows gleaming and front garden proud, the photo is blurred, as is her life and time.

Prints of forgotten holidays as life took it's toll on our best efforts, still to categorise and lay to rest inside albums thirty years past. There is a collection of once sparkling beach shells hauled home on a train in a rucksack, their colours fading with our images, never to return to the sea, but the sea once sang to them.

Grandparents and parents photographs contain people unknown to us in sepia single snapshots, distant lives in negative, somehow unconnected to us, obscure views with no name or date, captured on a first brownie. Triple prints, matted prints and glossed prints once arrived in exciting bright envelopes with negatives we would reprint and enlarge, "Would we, did we?" Those framed silk print enlargements we dreamed of, hung on still undecorated walls, three houses ago and still counting.

Who were these people before the camera, before the magic left them, still smiling, content, excited about life captured in these images. Bucket and spade clutched, towel rolled, hubby and granddad in suit and tie, turned up trousers defeating the waves, pipes in mouthes gripped, battling sea air on crab catch rocks and seagull swoop.

Even the colour photographs are fading of their best, cheap process, cheap times, cheap holidays abroad with everlasting sangria, concrete new towns, all in, jetted in, jetted out. 'My Holiday Album', with the smiles beaming sat on roped together donkeys, herded upward on a stony trail ducking Oleander trees as hats fell to the ground, how we laughed and camera clicked our Kodak and Polaroid instant, as we fell to the ground also.

The heavy 1970's patterned wallpaper merges with similar patterned tight jumpers, almost obscuring the children opening Christmas presents on a heavy patterned carpet, darkening the photographs lit only by struggling Christmas tree lights that are still bulbs. They shine onto a huge Tracy Island from Thunderbirds and a Tiny Tears doll that drinks a baby bottle then wets on the new carpet afterwards.

Life goes on from black and white, colour, movie, video and discs, we have taken less photographs in recent times in this year of blank. The older images and people could never foresee 2020, they could only guess of our future through their eyes through a camera lens, as we look back through the eye of a camera…that clicks and tricks us.

Yellow and White Iris

Yellow and white iris under the wind chimes looks
out from it's rooted pot
And sees the rainbows fading in windows crayoned
bright,
On pavements chalk drawn where heavy tread
stopped
And front gardens became tidy again,
The discarded latex gloves and face masks litter
changed lives
Clapping and chatting over fixed and painted fences,
Where once arguments ensued over bins and
bonfires, territory and overhang.
The pot of gold at rainbows end finally felled the
giants of commerce, squeezing the goose dry
And the beanstalk crumbled from it's cloud head
nodding, from real rainbows in the storm.
The cars are screeching past again, once courteous to
cyclists and pedestrians alike,
Walkers who had never walked, caught out by flip
flops and packed lunches
Walkers who had always walked, stout booted and
walking proud with twisted Gandalf staffs,
Cycle shops inundated with sales and repairs from
rusted garage and one day soon,